DEAR DEPRESSION

I'M BREAKING UP WITH YOU

Written By:
C'Era Dixon

© 2020 by
C'Era Dixon

All rights reserved. No part of this book may be reproduced in any form without permission in writing from the publisher, except in the case of brief quotations embodied in critical articles or reviews. No part of this publication may be reproduced, stored in a retrieval system, or transmitted in any form or by any means, electronic, mechanical, recording or otherwise, without the prior written permission of the author.

Scripture quotations are taken from the *Holy Bible*, New Living Translation, copyright ©1996, 2004, 2007 by Tyndale House Foundation; the *Holy Bible,* King James Version. New York: American Bible Society: 1999 Holy Bible, King James Version, copyright © 1999 by New York: Bible Society; and the *Holy Bible,* Amplified Version, *Copyright © 2015.*

Printed in the United States of America

THIS BOOK IS NOT INTENDED TO BE A HISTORY TEXT. While every effort has been made to check the accuracy of dates, locations, and historical information, no claims are made as to the accuracy of such information.

INFORMATION IN THIS BOOK DOES NOT REPRESENT THE VIEWS OF DUDLEY PUBLISHING HOUSE OR ANY OF IT'S SUBSIDAIRIES.
For book orders, author appearance inquires and interviews, contact author:

ISBN-13: 978-0-9988025-9-6

Dudley Publishing House
www.dudleypublishinghouse.net

Dedication

This book is dedicated to everyone who silently struggled with a mental illness and found peace their own way. May you all continue resting peacefully.

Acknowledgments

I want to first thank God for saving my life! Everything I am and have is because of His Grace, Mercy and Favor! Lord, I love you!

To Everyone who purchased this book, thank you! I hope you enjoy reading it and it touches your heart.

My Family: Thank you for your prayers, encouragement, sacrifices and support throughout this journey. When I needed you guys the most you were there without question or hesitation and I love you all tremendously.

Mommie: Our relationship hasn't always been perfect but I'm so glad it's getting better. You're the hardest working woman I know, I always wanted to give you something to be proud of since I didn't get a degree like you probably wanted. This is it! This is for you.

God Mother Tracy: I love you tremendously and admire your strength. You're forever u my thoughts and prayers. Sleep in peace Brit'ne

My Close Friends: Whitney, (My Bestie/Sis), Martika, Keyah, Monie, Kenua,

Alicia W., Ashley, La'Shonda, Zelda (Zee), Malcom, George, Latasha, Laryn, and Karyn. They're not enough words or time for me to tell you all individually what your friendships mean to me but thank you for loving me just as I am, for keeping all of my secrets, for being there for me all these years and never changing! Y'all are so amazing!! I love each of you.

My Better Me: You came into my life when nothing made sense. You've seen me at my worst but you still love me anyway. Thank you for staying up most nights until 3AM pushing me to finish this book. Thank you for allowing me to yell, vent and cry from frustration without judgment or interruption. Even when I wanted to quit you wouldn't let me and as you can see it paid off. I love you so much!

Pastor J & Session 3 Book Buddies: WE DID IT!!! Meeting you all was not an accident and I'm so grateful I was able to complete this amazing #WriteYourBookBootcamp with each of you. I could never forget you ladies. Love Ya'll!

Table of Contents

Mental Health Segment-...................pg.11

Introduction-..............................pg. 15

Chapter 1 – *How We Met*...................*pg17*

Chapter 2 – *Our First Date*.................*pg.25*

Chapter 3- *The Honeymoon Phase Lasted Too Long* *pg.33*

Chapter 4 – 2018, *I Almost Let Go*..........*pg.41*

Chapter 5 – *Team Jesus & Team*

Therapy..*pg.49*

Chapter 6 – *The Break-up: I've Got the*

Victory *pg.57*

Mental Health Segment

Last year I lost someone dear to me to suicide. He was well known in his community and church. He was always kindhearted and would give you his last to help. He had a great sense of humor and loved to joke. Outwardly he appeared to be fine but mentally he was suffering. His suicide awakened many people to include those who knew him through his church affiliations.

Mental health education is needed for the health of everyone. Suicide rates among children, teens, and young adults continue to rise. It is vitally important for the schools, churches, and communities to provide mental health education to the students, caregivers, and community members. It is okay to NOT be okay. We have to be willing and able to seek professional counsel to learn coping skills that will enable us to handle life when we are in a dark space.

I have personally known C'era since she was an infant. I've watched her overcome many insecurities and obstacles. She has become a very poised, hard working, and confident woman. I am thankful that she was able to overcome depression and I'm ecstatic that C'era decided to share her journey with us.
This book is needed to educate readers about mental health and help others who battle with

their psychological, emotional, and social well-being.

Karla L. Bradley, Ed.S.

Newport News, VA

Introduction

This book takes you on the journey of a young girl who struggles with depression and anxiety issues when she's bullied by classmates and sexually assaulted by the boys in her grandmother's neighborhood. As C'Era navigates through life trying to find her place in the world, she regretfully enters into a relationship with Depression. When her faith and strength are tested C'Era discovers she's not as strong as she often portrayed herself to be. Feeling alone and desperate for a permanent escape route, C'Era attempts to take her own life but is saved by the Holy Spirit. Dear Depression, I'm breaking up with you is an amazing read that taps into the mental health crisis the world is currently facing and offers Hope and Encouragement to the readers letting them know that they're not alone. If you or someone you know is battling with a mental illness don't be afraid to seek professional help!! Please call the Substance Abuse and Mental Health Services Administration Helpline at 1-800-662-HELP (4357).

1

How We Met

LIFE LESSON:

Don't Be Afraid to Express Yourself

I was born on May 3, 1988 in Norfolk, VA to a proud teenage mother Lavionia "Angel" Dixon. From 19 years old, until as long as I could remember, my mother worked anywhere from 2-3 jobs to make sure I had everything I wanted and needed. Due to my mom's work schedule, my grandmother who

I lovingly refer to as Mema, and my Aunts helped raise me. Mema lived in a neighborhood adjacent to our neighborhood, but the two neighborhoods were definitely polar opposites. At home I felt safe, secure, free and loved. But right across from there was a different experience that would leave me so broken inside. That place was called Wellington Oaks. There I experienced sadness and fearfulness from being bullied, terrorized, and sexually assaulted. I was always taught to tell an adult if someone hurt me "down there" but I kept my silence in exchange for my family's lives. They told me if I didn't say it was consensual they would kill all of us. Most of them were known gang members and I had no reason not to believe them. So, I haven't said a word until now.

I went to church with my Mema every Sunday, Tuesday and Thursday but still that just wasn't enough Jesus, Hallelujahs or "Lord I Need You" to save me from all that I would endure. I got into my first fight when I was 13. I remember her calling me an "ugly, black, tar baby". Before I knew it, I just blacked out. My mama always said words didn't hurt but, I'm sure, it's because nobody ever called her an "ugly, black, tar baby". I thought about her words and how much they affected me. Was she telling the truth?

Although, up until this point, no one had ever called me ugly, no one ever called me beautiful either. My mother nicknamed me her "Golden Girl" and in this moment I couldn't help but wonder why she never added beautiful to it. Was it because I was actually ugly after all? I remember telling my mom a girl called me ugly. She responded with, "C'Era, they talked about Jesus. Don't worry about those kids with no home training. They're just jealous of you." I was an only child so you know I was spoiled as all get out. I got everything on my Christmas list and 50 other things I didn't even think to ask for. My birthday parties were always extravagant and everybody in the neighborhood wanted to come because they knew Ms. Angel was going all out for her Golden Girl. I love my mother very much but I never told her how much that conversation affected me that day. I confided in her about someone calling me ugly and hurting my feelings. Even still, she never once told me I was beautiful or told me her words weren't true. To me, that meant they were. I felt like I was nothing more than an "ugly, black, tar baby".

Tears filled my eyes and I was overcome with emotion, so later that night I tried bleaching my skin to make it lighter, but that was unsuccessful. I tested one spot and sadly all it did was burn me making matters worse.

I didn't want to go outside. I had no desire to be around my friends. I locked myself in my room and starting planning my escape. Mama would call me for dinner but I didn't have an appetite. When she wasn't paying attention I'd throw my food away and head back to my room. I wasn't myself anymore. I was overwhelmed with so many emotions. I found myself full of anger, sadness, frustration, and hate. The worst one of them all though was DEPRESSION. Once DEPRESSION got a hold of me, I knew my life would never be the same.

Life Lesson 1:

Don't Be Afraid To Express Yourself

Life is definitely a continuous learning experience. As long as your learning then you're growing and growth is a great thing. It's important to know that everybody won't always understand what you're going through and that's okay. It doesn't mean that your feelings are insignificant. It's important to communicate with those around you and share your feelings. How can someone know how you feel if you don't tell them? Instead of expressing myself to my Mom I chose to keep my feelings inside and that only made matters worse. I should have immediately told her how I felt so she could address it. I later found out that my Mom didn't realize how the way she responded to our conversation hurt my feelings.

It's true that communication is key but communication alone isn't enough. It's our job to be effective communicators. With effective communication both parties should listen attentively, so that their message can be delivered clearly and each person feels heard and understood. So whether you choose to speak about it openly or write it in a letter, don't ever be afraid to express yourself. Your feelings matter, you matter!

2

Our First Date

LIFE LESSON:

SELF-LOVE IS NECESSARY

The first time my mother let me stay home alone for the weekend I was 2 weeks shy of my 15th birthday. Before she left, she gave me a lecture about having friends over and not opening the door for strangers. I barely had friends since we moved from our

2-bedroom apartment to a 3-bedroom single-family house over spring break. I can't say that I missed that place because I was happy to get away from all the drama. I dared anybody in my new neighborhood to try me. If they did, I was sure they wouldn't like the outcome. Sometimes I would look into the mirror and barely recognized myself.

I kissed my mother good-bye, practically pushing her out the door, and headed straight for the computer. I loved AOL Messenger and MySpace because I could be anybody I wanted to when I logged on. My profile consisted of pictures of all the beautiful women I wish I looked like. I also made sure my pages played the hottest R&B hit for the week. I hardly ever changed my "Top 8" friends list. I considered my friendship with those people to be as thick as thieves since elementary school. They never participated in the bullying or name calling. They weren't around when the madness happened so I had no reason to doubt our friendship.

While I was on messenger I received an instant messenger request from a user name I didn't quite recognize. I was always down for meeting new people so I accepted the request. It started off as friendly conversation, but eventually took a turn for the worst. Here I was minding my business, trying to enjoy my Friday night, and here comes the school bully accusing me of trying to have sex with her boyfriend. After all of the trauma I endured, boys were the absolute last thing on my mind. I hated all boys! We went back and forth for 10 minutes before she said the most horrific words that sent me into rage. She said, "Nobody is ever going to want you because you're too fat and too ugly." I stared at the screen for what seemed like an eternity. Tears filled my eyes as I gasped for air searching for the ultimate comeback, but I had nothing. I logged out of my computer and dropped to my knees crying hysterically. I replayed her words over in my head as if they were worthy of an encore. "You're too fat and too ugly." I repeated them over and over again. "You're too fat and too ugly." Each time placing a pill into my mouth, hoping, to permanently end my pain. That was the first night DEPRESSION took me on a date and, sadly, I knew it wouldn't be our last.

Life Lesson 2: Self-Love is Necessary

Self-love: regard for one's own well-being and happiness. There's no way you can truly love someone until you love yourself. When you hold yourself to a higher standard, you set the tone for how you want others to treat you. We all know that people can be cruel and words can hurt but only if you believe them. The lack of self-love will have you confused on who you truly are, so when people say things about you that aren't true you still believe them. A lot of the issues I experienced growing up was because of my lack of self-love. Not loving myself gave the wrong people access to treat me any way they wanted and I had to change that.

It's important to love yourself unconditionally, put yourself first when you can and speak positive affirmations to yourself daily. You should never apologize for being yourself or for someone else's inability to see just how awesome you are.

It's okay to give yourself a hug and take yourself on a date. Start a journal, write love letters to yourself. Self-love is more than just a feeling, it's a choice! And you have to always choose YOU, even when no one else does.

3

The Honeymoon Phase Lasted Too Long

LIFE LESSON:

KNOW WHEN TO WALK AWAY

One year after my first suicide attempt, I found myself with DEPRESSION, in love and inseparable. We were becoming more comfortable with each other and did everything thing together. I tried not to let my jealousy or self-consciousness ruin what we were building. We would drink together often. Even though I wasn't supposed to, DEPRESSION told me it was okay. At 16, I started stealing my mother's alcohol and putting it into my drinks. I'd be drunk by 5pm and vomiting around 6. My mom worked so much she hardly ever noticed. She was too busy sleeping from working long hours as a Fast- Track General Manager. I didn't mind because it gave DEPRESSION and me the opportunity to get closer.

She filled my head with so many lies but I believed her because, after all, she was my longest relationship and the most consistent. She never missed a beat. She made me feel happiness and sadness at the same time. She laughed at all my corny jokes. She made sure she never left me alone for more than 24 hours. She was really good at keeping my mind off of my reality. That's what you call a good partner. I thought I was lucky to have her in my life; she was all I knew the past few years. We got along great, honestly, but mostly because I didn't know who I was anymore. I felt like I had lost my purpose for living. I didn't have any reasons to smile anymore. My grades were dropping and I lost my desire to play sports. I just wanted to eat and sleep my days away. At this rate I felt no need to pray anymore because clearly God forgot to answer my first 10 prayers. At least, I thought He did, until He answered the first 5 at the same time.

It was senior year, graduation day, and this message was written inside one of the cards I opened on my way to the Ted Constant Convocation Center:

Dear C'Era,

You are beautiful. I created you in my image and you are not a mistake. I know sometimes the world can be cruel but I only gave you these tests because I was creating your testimony! You are beautiful. So let no one, not even depression or your own insecurities, tell you differently.

Love,

- *God*

Finally, the words I longed to hear came and at the perfect time. I was smiling from ear to ear because I went from being "too fat and too ugly" to "beautiful". I walked across that stage with my head held high, beaming with pride, excited for my new journey. I no longer walked around feeling like an ugly caterpillar. I finally felt like a beautiful butterfly. It felt good to smile again. Everyone noticed a difference; I felt so different. I was ready for adulthood and ready to unfold!

Life Lesson 3:
Know When To Walk Away

A lot of times we stay in situations that are toxic because we're comfortable. It's important not to allow your comfortability to cloud your judgment. In life we will have choices to make and those choices will come with consequences.

Walking away from toxic situations can be difficult but often times staying can cause more harm than good. You have to find the courage to walk away, even if that means you have to be alone. Never feel obligated to stay in a situation that threatens your self-worth, self-respect or peace of mind.

It's okay to give chances but God doesn't want us to be foolish. Don't wait for someone to realize your worth and value. Realize it yourself and move on. And in moving on be sure to give yourself time to heal from those previous situations that broke you.

Remember, God will always take care of you. Just trust His plan for your life.

4

2018, I Almost Let Go

LIFE LESSON:

YOU DESERVE TO LIVE

After high school I bounced around trying to find my place in the world, still unsure of my purpose. I found myself in New London, Connecticut sleeping on my best friends couch. There, I eventually got on my feet and landed a job with AT&T. Here I am 10 years later, packing my car for my move to New Bern, NC. I thought moving to the country would give me a permanent sense of peace and happiness. I strategically picked the perfect neighborhood, layout, and location for the best commute because I didn't want anything to get in the way of my perfect new beginning.

    Two months into my move I was dealing with a bad breakup. Two months after that, I lost the most amazing soul I've ever known to suicide. Ernesto's passing hit me like a ton of bricks. Not only because we made a promise that he would help me bring life into this world, but also because I was jealous.

The eternal peace that I had been searching for, he finally received. He no longer had to deal with the ugliness of the world and I envied him. After all I had been through, I wish it had been me. I found myself slowly breaking and, although I only moved 3 hours away from home, I couldn't get any visitors. I know I said I wanted peace, but where was the love? The weekly phone calls stopped. The text messages went unanswered for weeks. All I was left with were my thoughts at 2 a.m. Depression slowly made her way back into my bedroom. Tears stained my pillows as I searched for a way out. I didn't think anybody would miss me.

At this point, it's been 5 months of nothing so, I began to put my plan into action. I went to work everyday and acted as if I was okay, but truthfully, I was slowly dying inside. I started to write letters to my loved ones explaining why I knew suicide was the answer to my forever happiness: my peace. I already had two failed attempts so I needed this one to work. I strategically planned everything out; even down to the day I would say my final good-byes. Finally, the day had arrived I made my rounds calling and texting those with my normal "I'm just checking on you" message so nothing would seem out of place. I learned that day, that Kate Spade my favorite designer committed suicide earlier that month and soon I would join her and others like us.

    I took one final scroll on Facebook and Instagram and as I was getting the rope ready to tie around my neck I received a direct message from a friend. She begin to tell me that I had purpose, value, that I was enough, that I mattered, that God loved me, and He wanted me to stay here and help pull others out of their darkness. She said that suicide wasn't the answer and the peace I was searching for was inside me all along. She reminded me that life happens. Although people have good intentions sometimes they genuinely forget to call and check in but that doesn't mean we are insignificant to them. How did she know exactly what was on my heart and what I was planning to do, just minutes before? I never told anybody what my plans were, but she knew and she begged me not to go through with them. We texted for hours and I laid in the fetal position crying on my living room floor knowing for the first time in my life God really had Angels in human form looking out for His people. I almost let go that day but He saved me so that I could save others.

Life Lesson 4:

You Deserve To Live

Depression can cause you to have suicidal thoughts but it's important to know that you matter and you deserve to live! Don't ever forget that. Life maybe hard but you are strong enough to get through it. Remember that your family and friends aren't perfect and they're definitely not mind readers. Be sure to communicate with them how you're feeling, even if they don't always reach out first. Their absence doesn't mean that they don't care about you, they could be dealing with their own personal issues but always know you can still reach out for help if you need it.

If you're having suicidal thoughts please reach out to a family member, friend, mental health counselor or call the National Suicide Prevention Line at 1-800-273-8255. If you prefer to text then you can send TALK to 741741.

5

Team Jesus &

Team Therapy

LIFE LESSON:

WE NEED JESUS & THERAPY

If I may be honest, that last incident was an eye-opener for me. The devil really got into my mind and I almost took my own life. I still get chills thinking about it. Throughout this whole situation I realized, even though I turned my back on God, He still loved me. Through all of my mess, He still decided to save me. I didn't want to worry my family with all that was going on down here so I decided to call my Mema just to check in and get prayer. My Mema is an Evangelist at Bibleway Holiness Church in Chesapeake, VA. She's saved, sanctified and filled with the tongue talking Holy Ghost, so if anybody knew how to reach God on my behalf she could. Growing up I always joked about her prayers reaching Him first.

"Hello My Oldest Granddaughter." she answered. Mema always knew how to put a smile on my face. "Mema, I'm homesick and I need you to pray for me, things aren't going too good." I didn't want her to worry too much, or ask too many questions, but I wanted to make sure she knew how desperately I needed God back in my life. I was always taught to pray about everything and worry about nothing. No one ever told me what to do when it seemed my prayers weren't being answered. No one said what to do if I ever felt like God had forgotten about me. They left that part out.

When Mema finished her prayer, I felt like a weight had been lifted off of my heart. Her prayers had that type of effect on you.

She gave me some scriptures to read before we hung up the phone. As the weeks went by I started reading my bible more, praying more, fasting and rebuilding my relationship with God. If anybody could bring me out of this darkness, He could. I just had to keep going to church, keep praying, keep reading my bible and He would take care of me.

I was scrolling on Facebook when I came across a post from a friend who was posting about needing a good therapist in her area. What could a therapist do that Jesus couldn't, I thought to myself. Curiosity got the best of me and for the next 2 hours I asked google every question I was ashamed to post on Facebook. I came across so many articles about free programs depending on where you worked and I made it my business the next day to inquire if AT&T had a program. Thankfully they did and I was able to set up an appointment for professional help. I was so nervous at my first appointment. I didn't want to say too much and I didn't want to say too little but I was so proud of me for recognizing that I needed help that extended beyond my faith.

I was able to break generational curses of silence. The often used saying of, "what goes on in this house stays in this house" no longer mattered. I cried, I yelled, I screamed, I wrote and most importantly, I persevered. With each session, I learned more and more about myself. I was able to express my feelings without being judged, cut off mid-sentence, or simply ignored. Therapy helped me to cope with life's hardships and adversities and also improved my overall productivity and effectiveness at work and with my loved ones. This breakthrough was so necessary and I owed it to myself to make sure I was completely healed and whole mentally. I received mental and emotional healing with the help of God & therapy. It's not too late for you to start your healing process. Let's normalize therapy together.

Life Lesson 5:

We Need Jesus & Therapy

Growing up in the church I always felt that I didn't need to seek any professional help because God was all I needed. There was also a negative stigma in the black community centered around talking to a mental health professional. It was something that we just didn't do. It wasn't until my 3rd suicide attempt that I realized I needed Jesus and a therapist.

I had to learn that it was okay to talk to a therapist and God. In order to heal from our past traumas some of us are going to need prayer and a professional. It doesn't mean that your Faith is compromised, you've just added another solution to help you navigate through life. I honestly feel that both Faith and Therapy can work together and that doesn't make you less of a Christian for seeking that much needed help.

Therapy helped me find healing emotionally and mentally. I learned things about myself that I never would've without it. God will always be my Hope, Strength, Comforter and my Provider. I will always trust in Him and continue to pray my way through life's struggles. I also find comfort in knowing I have Him and my therapist on my side.

6

The Break-up...I've Got the Victory

THE FINAL LESSON:

NEVER GO BACKWARDS

Dear Depression,

We need to talk! We've spent the last 18 years together and if I let this relationship go on any longer I'd only be doing a disservice to myself. You came into my life when I was vulnerable, empty, broken and struggling with self-esteem issues. You pretended to love me but all you did was use me for your own pleasures. You fed me lies, tried to convince me to take my own life, stained my pillows and made me feel I was unworthy and incapable of genuine love. I thought you wanted what was best for me but I started to notice if someone tried to get close to me you'd use my insecurities to eventually run them off, leaving me stuck with you. You told me that you loved me, but the way you treat me isn't how you treat someone you love. The other week you laughed in my face when I tried to tell you it was over. You said I was stuck and that I'd never find anyone else quite like you. I smiled excitedly because at this point the thought of you makes me vomit.

Depression, you were so wrong about me! I am beautiful. I love who I see in the mirror. I am worthy, I am enough, I have value, I have purpose and I do deserve happiness and genuine love! I will no longer allow you to make me feel sad, empty, hopeless, and worthless or consume my mind with suicidal thoughts. We are OVER! Please don't try and contact me once you receive this letter. I've been instructed by my therapist to permanently end all contact. I MATTER and I refuse to let my story END!

You did everything in your power to break me but I've got the VICTORY!

Signed,

Healed, Delivered and Set Free

P.S. I now cast you back to the pits of HELL and command you to shrivel up and die in the mighty name of Jesus!!

The Final Lesson:

Never Go Backwards

There's going to be times when loneliness creeps in and you're going to want to go back to that situation that initially broke you but don't. You have to think about how far you've come and how unhappy you felt in that situation. Is one temporary moment of happiness worth all the sacrifices you had to make to finally find your peace? The answer is No. Going back to a situation that broke you will only hurt you more in the long run. Know your worth and never compromise it for anyone.

You probably thought you wouldn't survive that situation that nearly killed you but here you are living; existing.

Dear Depression, we're breaking up with you and going back just isn't an option.

Thoughts & Reflections:

About the Author

C'Era Dixon is an author who lives in Raleigh, NC but calls the Hampton Roads (757) area of Virginia home. She used her experiences with childhood trauma, depression and anxiety and became a Mental Health Advocate in 2018. She brought awareness to the worlds mental health crisis through her social media platforms. With 3700+ followers as her audience, C'Era is advocating for the mind of others and helping break generational curses. In the fall of 2019 C'Era completed Dudley's Publishing House

#WriteYourBookBootcamp with the infamous #BookBully Jasmine Dudley! In 2019, she wrote her own autobiography, Her book is titled *Dear Depression, I'm Breaking Up With You.* C'Era is a member of Praise Temple Apostolic Faith Church. She enjoys pure authentic worship, singing, concerts, comedy shows, bowling, reading books and traveling. When she's not working her full-time job she loves to volunteer in the community.

C'era Dixon

www.facebook.com/iamceradixon/

IG: @iamceradixon

iamceradixon@gmail.com

www.ingramcontent.com/pod-product-compliance
Lightning Source LLC
LaVergne TN
LVHW041458070426
835507LV00009B/666